Library of Congress Control Number: 2017935600

Designed by Justin Watkinson
Type set in Impact/Minion Pro/Univers LT Std

All photos are from the collections of the US National Archives and Records Administration unless otherwise noted.

ISBN: 978-0-7643-5419-9
Printed in China

Published by Schiffer Publishing, Ltd.
4880 Lower Valley Road
Atglen, PA 19310
Phone: (610) 593-1777; Fax: (610) 593-2002
E-mail: Info@schifferbooks.com
www.schifferbooks.com

For our complete selection of fine books on this and related subjects, please visit our website at www.schifferbooks.com. You may also write for a free catalog.

This book may be purchased from the publisher.
Please try your bookstore first.

We are always looking for people to write books on new and related subjects. If you have an idea for a book, please contact us at proposals@schifferbooks.com.

Schiffer Publishing's titles are available at special discounts for bulk purchases for sales promotions or premiums. Special editions, including personalized covers, corporate imprints, and excerpts can be created in large quantities for special needs. For more information, contact the publisher.

Acknowledgments

As with all of my projects, this book would not have been possible without the generous help of many friends. Instrumental to the completion of this book were Tom Kailbourn, Dana Bell, Scott Taylor, Stan Piet, the staff and volunteers at the National Museum of Naval Aviation, Doug Siegfried with the Tailhook Association, and Robert Hanshew with the Naval History and Heritage Command. Most importantly, I am grateful for the help and support of my wife Denise.

Contents

Introduction

The aircraft that came to be the Douglas TBD was spawned by a 1934 Bureau of Aeronautics request for proposals for a new torpedo bomber. With the Navy's array of Martin BM-2 and Great Lakes TG-2 biplane torpedo bombers growing long in the tooth, and a four-ship addition to the carrier force planned, a new, modern torpedo bomber was desired. The specifications issued provided that the aircraft was to be powered by the newly developed Pratt & Whitney 800 horsepower XR-1830-60 14-cylinder twin-row radial aircraft engine, dubbed the Twin Wasp. Further specified was that the aircraft be capable of delivering a Mk.XIII aerial torpedo to its target, or alternately three 500-pound bombs or a combination of 500- and 100-pound bombs.

Three responses to the request for proposal were received. One, from the Bristol, Pennsylvania-based Hall Aluminum Aircraft Corporation, while test-flown, was unsuccessful. The twin-engine floatplane, designated XPTBH-2, did not lend itself to carrier operations. While retained by the Navy and used until destroyed by a hurricane in 1938, the aircraft was not given serious consideration. Two years later Hall Aluminum Aircraft was bought by Consolidated Aircraft.

A second response, this from Great Lakes Aircraft, offered a new biplane. Known as the XTBG-1, this aircraft would be the final biplane torpedo bomber given consideration by the US Navy. Unfortunately for Great Lakes, testing of the prototype by the Navy showed the aircraft to have poor performance and unstable flight characteristics. Great Lakes would also create the equally lackluster XB2G-1, a biplane dive bomber offered as an improvement to their BG-1 dive bomber. The XB2G-1 was not placed into production, and Great Lakes would cease operations in 1936.

Douglas Aircraft Company's proposed aircraft won favor, and a prototype was ordered. However, before the prototype was completed, Douglas further refined the design, the resulting aircraft being an all-metal monoplane with hydraulically folding wings. This was the first time that power assistance had been used in folding wings. The XTBD-1, as the Douglas design was designated, also featured a totally enclosed cockpit, which along with the power-fold wings, main landing wheel brakes, and all-metal construction were firsts for naval aircraft.

The TBD-1 was designed to replace the US Navy's two operational torpedo bombers of the early and mid-1930s, the Martin BM-2 and, here, the Great Lakes TG-2, in Torpedo Squadron 2 markings. Both were biplanes with open cockpits and fabric-covered wings. *San Diego Air and Space Museum*

Douglas Aircraft of Santa Monica, California, constructed a wooden mock-up of the XTBD-1, its proposed design for a US Navy Bureau of Aeronautics requirement for a new torpedo plane issued in mid-1934. A real engine was installed in the mock-up. *National Museum of Naval Aviation*

The XTBD-1 mock-up included wooden propeller blades and frame members and plywood skin. Two bombs were mounted on the belly of the fuselage, and what was probably meant to represent a gun camera was on fittings adjacent to the windscreen. *National Archives and Records Administration*

Although the XTBD-1 mock-up was supported by two stands, it had a retractable main landing gear. In this photo dated March 24, 1934, the starboard landing gear has been lowered and the starboard wing has been folded. The wheel is represented by a frame. *National Archives and Records Administration*

In a photo taken the same day as the preceding two views, the port wing has not yet been installed on the XTBD-1 mock-up. The tail wheel was retractable. Visible through the frame of the fuselage are the seats for the three crewmen and other components. *National Archives and Records Administration*

The tail wheel is extended on the XTBD-1 mock-up. Protruding from the windscreen is the pilot's telescopic gun sight. Slung underneath the fuselage is a mock-up of an aerial torpedo, with its nose angled down from the longitudinal centerline of the plane. *National Archives and Records Administration*

CHAPTER 1

The XTBD-1

The Douglas XTBD-1 prototype first flew on April 15, 1935. It was assigned Bureau Number (abbreviated BuNo: this was the USN serial number) 9720. Initially, as seen in this photograph dated July 12, 1935, the XTBD-1 had a low-profile canopy. The XTBD-1 featured an all-metal semimonocoque fuselage with fabric-covered control surfaces. Powering the aircraft was a Pratt & Whitney XR-1830-60 radial engine rated at 800 horsepower. The three-man crew consisted of the pilot, the assistant pilot/bombardier, and the radioman/gunner seated in tandem. *National Museum of Naval Aviation*

The new Douglas torpedo bomber first took to the air on April 15, 1935. After initial flight tests, on April 24, the aircraft was ferried from the Santa Monica, California plant to the Anacostia Naval Air Station in Washington, DC. Performance trials of the aircraft began almost immediately, and were followed by night flight testing at Naval Air Station Norfolk beginning June 13. From July until September 20, 1935, the aircraft underwent bombing tests at the Naval Proving Ground Dahlgren in Virginia. After a maintenance period at Anacostia, the XTBD-1 was again flown to Norfolk, this time for torpedo drop tests.

After another transcontinental fight, carrier suitability trials began aboard the USS *Lexington* (CV-2) and Naval Air Station North Island in California on December 5, 1935. In total, there were thirteen launch and landing cycles aboard the *Lexington*, with those tests concluding December 10. For these flights Lt. William V. Davis, Lt. Stewart Ingerson, and Lt. (JG) George Anderson alternated turns at the controls.

While pleased with the performance of the aircraft overall, these trials did point to some improvements that should be made prior to series production. Chief among these were a larger canopy, which would allow for the inclusion of rollover protection, as well as improved visibility and crew comfort. Concurrently, the oil cooler was relocated from the bottom of the cowling to beneath the starboard wing, and the carburetor air intake on the port side of the cowl was deleted.

Subsequently, the aircraft was accepted by the Navy and began accelerated service testing. These tests spanned from February 23 through April 10, 1937. At the conclusion of those tests, the XTBD-1 lived out the rest of its life as a test subject at Pratt & Whitney, and again in the hands of the Navy, being used for armament installation tests in Philadelphia. Its final service was as an instructional airframe at Norman, Oklahoma, where it was finally scrapped on September 10, 1943.

The original canopy of the XTBD-1 was not much higher than the top of the turtle deck, aft of the canopy, and it gave little headroom to the crew, particularly the pilot. Marked on the vertical fin is the Bureau Number, 9720; on the rudder is marked "XTBD-1." *San Diego Air and Space Museum*

The wings are extended on the XTBD-1. It was necessary to have foldable wings on a carrier-based aircraft with a large wingspan—in this case, fifty feet—in order to fit planes on the flight deck, elevators, and the hangar deck. The XTBD-1's wings were folded hydraulically. *San Diego Air and Space Museum*

The wings are folded on the XTBD-1. The main landing gear shock, or oleo, struts were painted white, with shiny steel pistons adjacent to the wheels. A diagonal undercarriage leg strut on the outboard side of each shock strut gave extra rigidity to the landing gear. *San Diego Air and Space Museum*

The design of the wing bulkheads at the wing-fold line of the XTBD-1 is apparent. Two bombs are mounted below the fuselage. The scoop-shaped structure in the shadows below and aft of the cowl is the oil cooler housing. The cowl flaps are shown open. *San Diego Air and Space Museum*

The pilot and assistant pilot/bombardier of the XTBD-1 are looking at the photographer through their open canopies during a test flight. The oil cooler housing is more visible from this angle. Protruding below the starboard wing is the main landing gear wheel. *San Diego Air and Space Museum*

On November 4, 1936, a series of documentary photos was taken of the XTBD-1, BuNo 9720. The new, higher canopy had been installed by this date. There was an abrupt angle between the bottom of the cowl and the bottom of the forward fuselage. This feature later would be redesigned with the TBD-1, with a more or less straight profile from the front of the cowl to the belly of the fuselage between the wings. This redesign would be applied to the TBD-1. *National Archives and Records Administration*

A Navy pilot puts the XTBD-1 through its paces on October 14, 1935, during a period when the plane had completed its torpedo-dropping tests and was about to begin carrier trials. Sitting in the rear seats are two sailors wearing enlisted men's white caps. *National Museum of Naval Aviation*

In another of the ongoing modifications undertaken on the XTBD-1 in this period, the oil cooler had been removed from the rear of the cowl and had been placed inside the starboard wing; the slot below the anti-slip walkway on the wing formed its air intake. *National Archives and Records Administration*

The angle of the wings when folded is portrayed in this photo. Just below the leading edge of the port wing forward of the landing gear in the slight bulge was the landing light, with a clear, round lens. The main landing gear tires were smooth-tread. *National Archives and Records Administration*

Visible through the canopy aft of the pilot's cockpit is the rollover pylon, a crew-safety feature that was added when the heightened canopy was installed. It had two diagonal braces that were wide apart at their bottoms but met at the top of the headrest. *National Archives and Records Administration*

The wings and horizontal stabilizers of the XTBD-1 had corrugated aluminum-alloy skins, which enhanced their strength. This feature carried over to the production TBD-1. Radio antenna masts were now present atop the vertical fin and ahead of the cockpit. *National Archives and Records Administration*

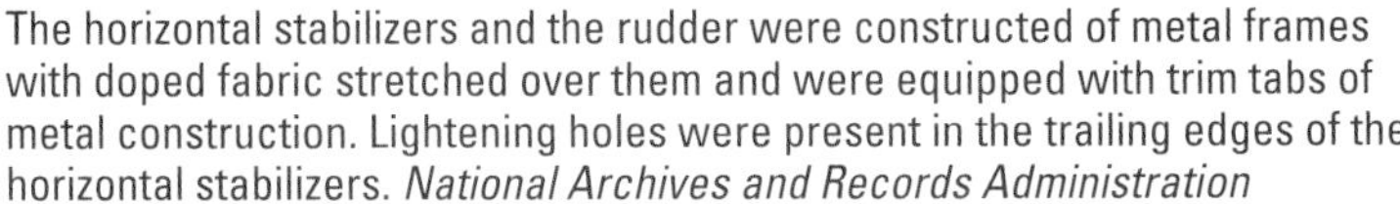
The horizontal stabilizers and the rudder were constructed of metal frames with doped fabric stretched over them and were equipped with trim tabs of metal construction. Lightening holes were present in the trailing edges of the horizontal stabilizers. *National Archives and Records Administration*

The engine cowl comprised, front to rear, the nose ring, the removable cowl panels with a horizontal piano hinge between them, and the cowl flaps. Aft of the cowl flaps was the engine-accessories compartment, the hinged access panels for which are shown open. *National Archives and Records Administration*

On each side of the XTBD-1 was a carburetor air intake over a non-moving panel in line with the cowl flaps above the engine exhaust stub. By the time this photo was taken on November 4, 1936, a streamlined fairing had been added to the rear of each intake. *National Archives and Records Administration*

As seen on the starboard side of the cowl with the flaps open, the panel adjacent to the front of the carburetor intake was immobile. The access panel with the carburetor intake fairing affixed to it is different in shape than the corresponding one on the opposite side. *National Archives and Records Administration*

With the cowl and engine-accessories compartment panels removed, the reason for the elongated access panel indicated in the preceding photo is apparent: the panel covered the bay for a fixed .30-caliber machine gun; its mount is the bar with the lightening holes. *National Archives and Records Administration*

With the port-side panels removed, the engine and the engine-accessories compartment, including the diagonal tubes of the engine support, are visible. The port carburetor intake scoop had a different look when the panel with its streamlined fairing was removed. *National Archives and Records Administration*

In a view forward from the cockpit of the XTBD-1, at the bottom is the windscreen, to the front of which is the oil tank, with the filler cap to the right. The open cowl flaps reveal the exhaust collector ring. At the top is the Pratt & Whitney XR-1830-60. *National Archives and Records Administration*

The XTBD-1's Pratt & Whitney XR-1830-60 engine was an air-cooled radial design with fourteen cylinders arranged in two rows. Each of the Hamilton Standard constant-speed propeller's blades had an oval-shaped manufacturer's logo decal and a data plate. *National Archives and Records Administration*

The second model of the cockpit canopy of the XTBD-1 with its sections closed is observed from the port side. It comprised seven sections, three of which were fixed and four of which slid on rails when opened. The rollover pylon is also visible inside. *National Archives and Records Administration*

The canopy of the XTBD-1 is displayed in the open position. The pilot's section slid to the rear, with its front tilted on the rails in a raised position. The assistant pilot/bombardier's section slid to the rear, and the radioman's two sections slid forward in a stacked configuration. *National Archives and Records Administration*

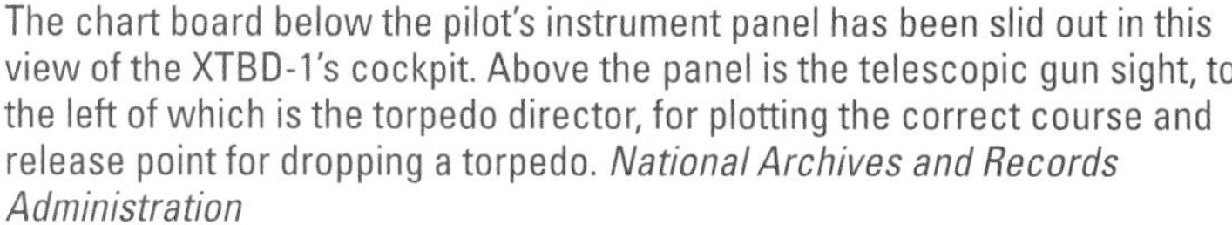

The chart board below the pilot's instrument panel has been slid out in this view of the XTBD-1's cockpit. Above the panel is the telescopic gun sight, to the left of which is the torpedo director, for plotting the correct course and release point for dropping a torpedo. *National Archives and Records Administration*

On the cockpit's starboard console is the long handle for the manual hydraulic pump, along with wing-flap, parking-brake, wing-fold, and landing-gear controls. The hand crank above the console operated the canopy; to the front of it is the gun-charging handle. *National Archives and Records Administration*

The instrument panel is displayed with the chart board stored. The instrument panel comprised an upper and a lower section that was positioned ahead of the upper one. At the center is the control stick; the brake treadles atop the rudder pedals are at the bottom. *National Archives and Records Administration*

With the seat removed from the cockpit for this photo, at the upper center is the throttle quadrant, below which is an electrical control panel. The wheels next to that panel controlled the rudder trim tab and the elevator trim tabs. To the top left is a canopy track. *National Archives and Records Administration*

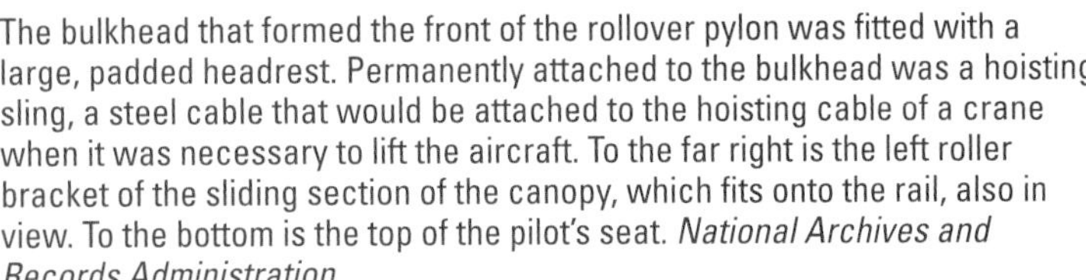

The bulkhead that formed the front of the rollover pylon was fitted with a large, padded headrest. Permanently attached to the bulkhead was a hoisting sling, a steel cable that would be attached to the hoisting cable of a crane when it was necessary to lift the aircraft. To the far right is the left roller bracket of the sliding section of the canopy, which fits onto the rail, also in view. To the bottom is the top of the pilot's seat. *National Archives and Records Administration*

Looking into the pilot's cockpit from the port side, the absence of the seat makes it possible to see extra features in the bombardier's station on the lower deck in the bottom of the fuselage. Toward the left are the rears of the doors for the bombardier's window; these are perforated with lightening holes. Toward the center is the bombardier's kneeling pad. The object with the round opening in it between the kneeling pad and the doors for the bombardier's window is the bombsight mount. *National Archives and Records Administration*

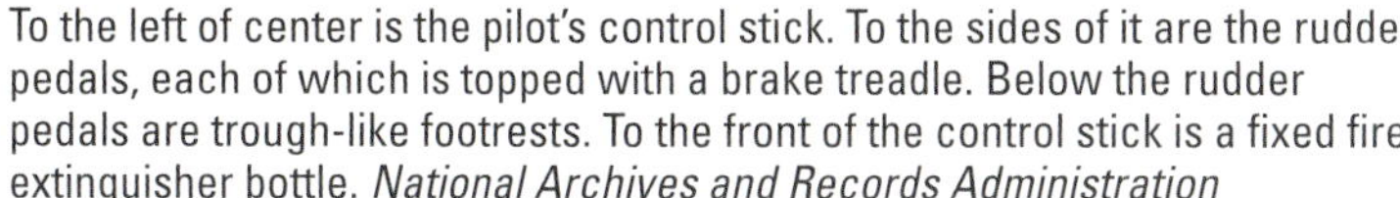

To the left of center is the pilot's control stick. To the sides of it are the rudder pedals, each of which is topped with a brake treadle. Below the rudder pedals are trough-like footrests. To the front of the control stick is a fixed fire extinguisher bottle. *National Archives and Records Administration*

As seen in a view of the port side of the assistant pilot's cockpit, the footrests were hinged and could be folded up. On the console at the center is the hand crank for manually starting the engine. A rudimentary throttle control is at the top of the photo. *National Archives and Records Administration*

The assistant pilot sat in the center cockpit when not engaged as bombardier on the lower deck. To the left is his small instrument panel, below which is his starboard rudder pedal with a folding pedal. At the center is a CO_2 bottle for inflating wing flotation bags. *National Archives and Records Administration*

TBD Devastator	
Wingspan	50 feet
Length	35 feet
Height	15 feet, 1 inch
Max Weight	9,862 pounds
Powerplant	Pratt &Whitney R-1830-64
Cylinders	14
Horsepower	900
Max Speed	206 MPH
Service Ceiling	19,700 feet
Range	700 miles
Crew	3
Armament	1 x .30-caliber or 1 x .50-caliber fixed machine gun; one .30-caliber flexible MG; 1,200 lbs. of bombs, or one torpedo.

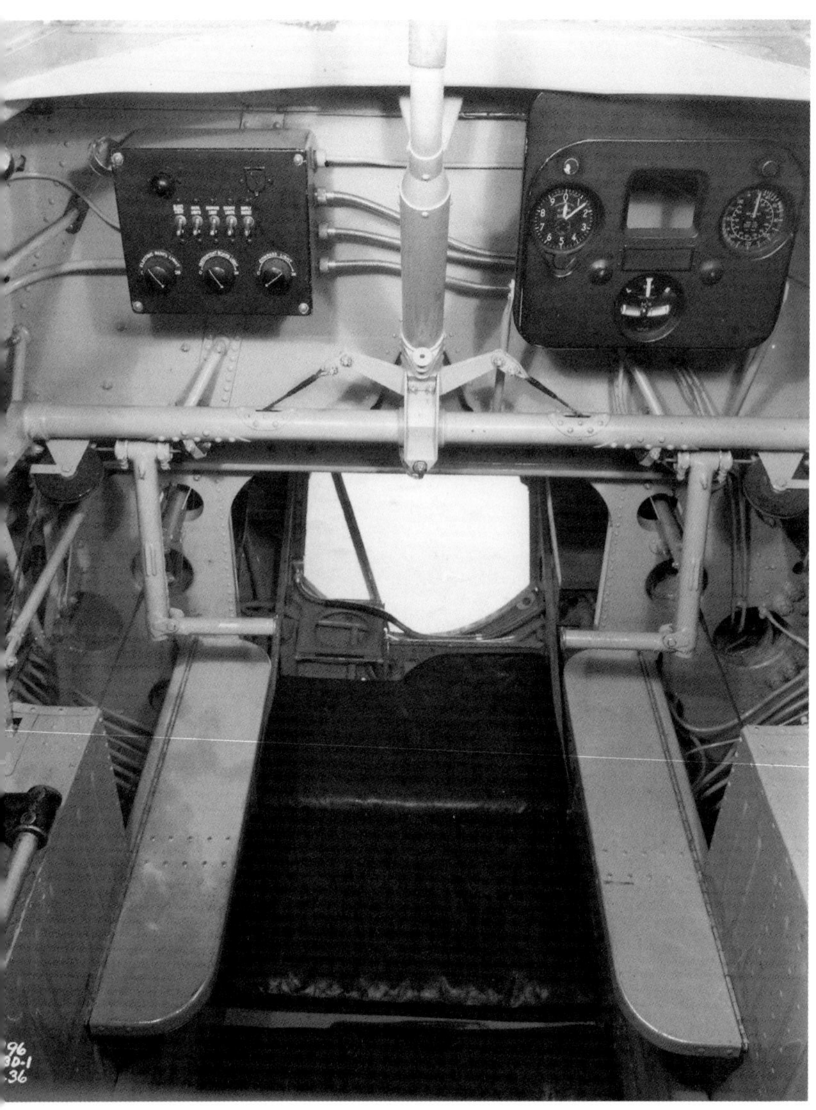

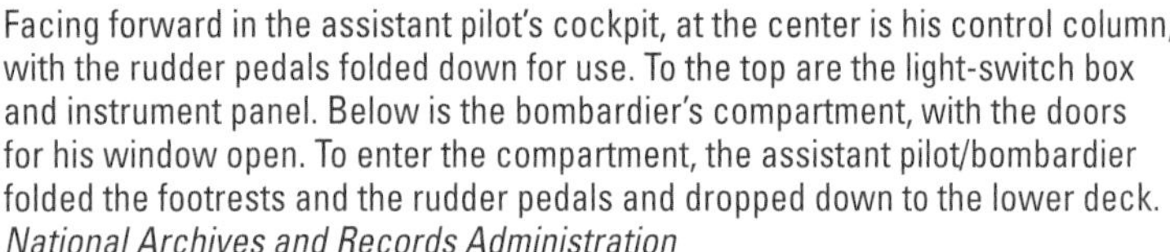

Facing forward in the assistant pilot's cockpit, at the center is his control column, with the rudder pedals folded down for use. To the top are the light-switch box and instrument panel. Below is the bombardier's compartment, with the doors for his window open. To enter the compartment, the assistant pilot/bombardier folded the footrests and the rudder pedals and dropped down to the lower deck. *National Archives and Records Administration*

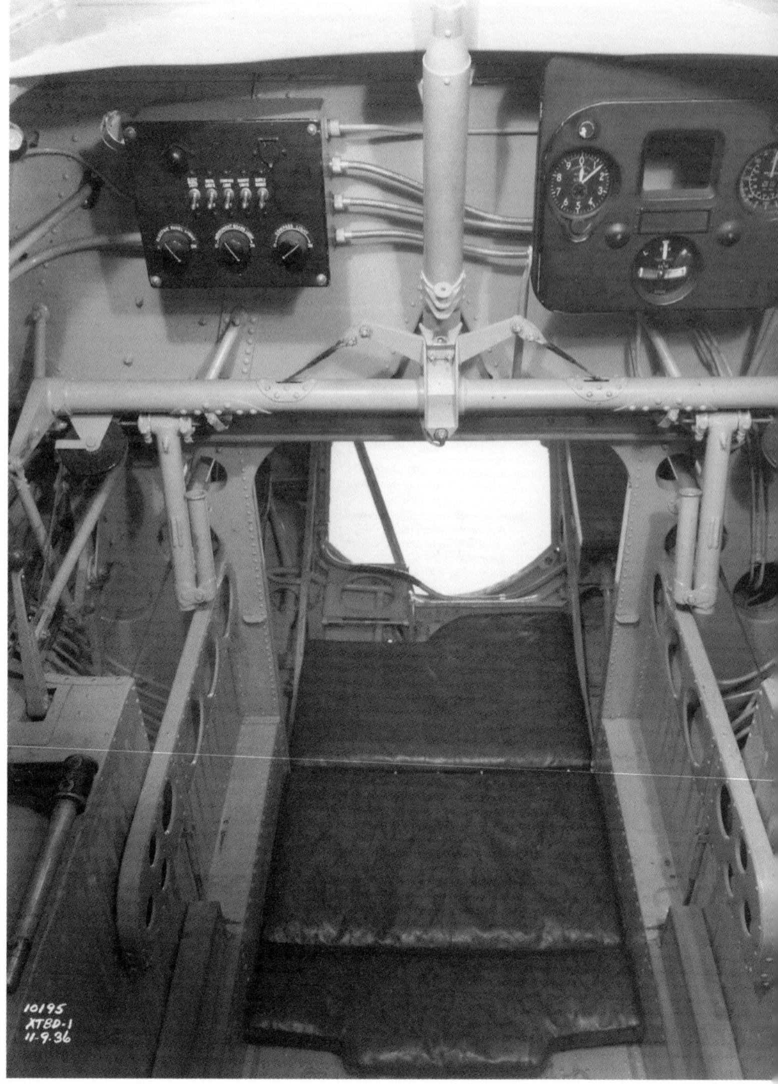

In a companion view to the preceding photo, the rudder pedals and the footrests in the assistant pilot/bombardier's cockpit have been folded. The bombardier's aiming window is visible below; it has an angled frame member. The extent of the bombardier's kneeling pad is apparent. To the left front of the pad is the bombsight mount. The manner in which the control column is mounted on a lateral tube is shown. *National Archives and Records Administration*

Viewed from under the forward end of the fuselage looking aft are the open doors for the bombardier's window. Each door was hung from two hinges. The window, consisting of two panes with a diagonal frame separating them, was located in a well above the doors. *National Archives and Records Administration*

The radioman/gunner's cockpit of the XTBD-1, viewed from the starboard side in an October 19, 1936, photo, had an unfinished look, with mock-ups of some components present, and the radio equipment and shelving was different than in the preceding photo. *National Archives and Records Administration*

The radio installation at the front of the radioman/gunner's cockpit was photographed on April 11, 1935, eleven days before its first flight. On top of the radio rack was a radio direction finder (RDF) loop antenna and, to the left of it, a radio transmitter key. *National Archives and Records Administration*

Another photo from October 19, 1936, shows the radioman/gunner's cockpit from a low angle, facing forward toward the radio equipment. To the left is the reel for a trailing antenna. To the lower right is an electrical panel. At the center is the transmitter. *National Archives and Records Administration*

The entire canopy had been removed in this October 19, 1936, photo taken from the radioman/gunner's compartment. To the right of the shelf holding the transmitter key and the RDF antenna is the radio control unit, with volume and selector controls on it. *National Archives and Records Administration*

In an April 11, 1935, photo, the radioman/gunner's seat rests in the Browning .30-caliber machine gun ring mount in the XTBD-1. Each side of the ring rested in a pivot mount. When not in use, the machine gun was stored in a recess with top doors in the turtle deck. *National Archives and Records Administration*

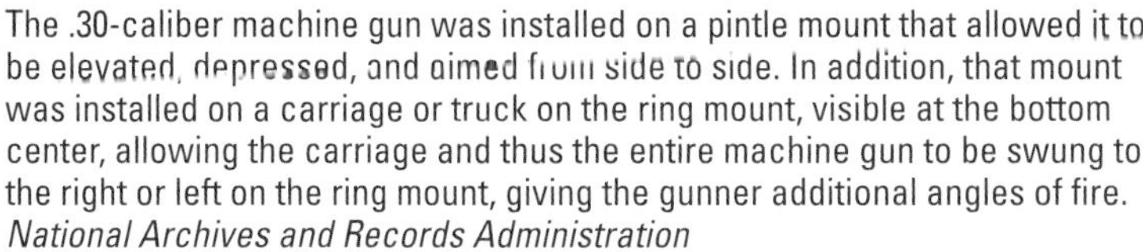

The .30-caliber machine gun was installed on a pintle mount that allowed it to be elevated, depressed, and aimed from side to side. In addition, that mount was installed on a carriage or truck on the ring mount, visible at the bottom center, allowing the carriage and thus the entire machine gun to be swung to the right or left on the ring mount, giving the gunner additional angles of fire. *National Archives and Records Administration*

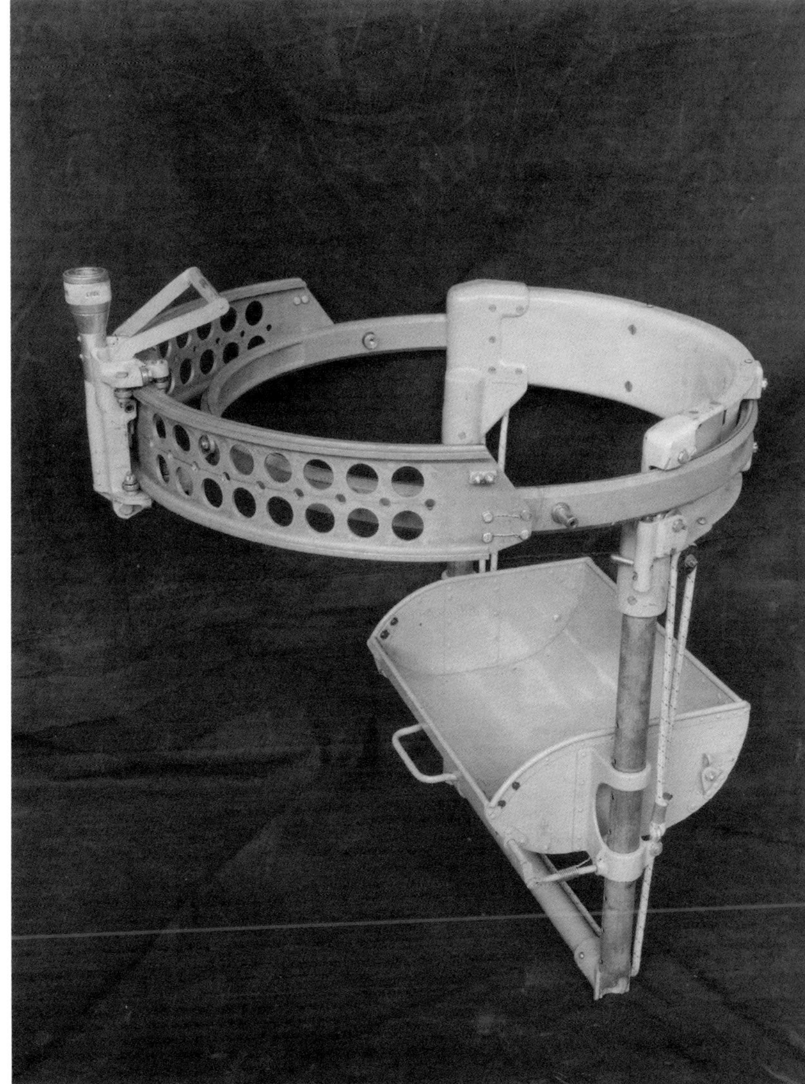

The ring mount and seat are shown dismounted. The seat could be traversed in the ring mount so the radioman could face forward or aft. The seat bucket was adjustable in height. The track for the gun carriage is perforated with lightening holes. To the left is the carriage, with pintle socket and triangular-shaped carriage locking handle. The gunner could tilt the ring mount and seat for an optimal angle of fire. *National Archives and Records Administration*

The port main landing gear of the XTBD-1 is displayed in its extended position. The main strut was the Bendix Pneudraulic model, an oleo-type shock strut in which a piston acted with oil and air inside the strut to achieve shock-buffering. A Bendix data plate is visible toward the top of the strut. Outboard of the shock strut was a diagonal side brace, and to the rear was a rear brace. *National Archives and Records Administration*

The port landing gear is shown in the retracted position. When retracted, the wheels remained partially exposed below the wing. Cutouts in the wing accommodated the shock strut and the side brace, each of which has a streamlined fairing for its pivot mechanism. *National Archives and Records Administration*

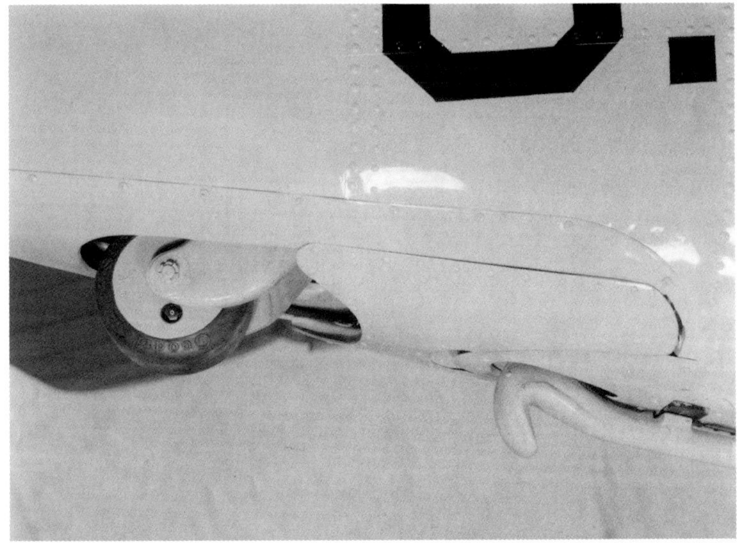

The tail wheel on the XTBD-1 was retractable and is shown in the retracted position from starboard. The tire was a Goodrich Silvertown. A fairing covered the front of the landing gear bay when the wheel was retracted. To the right is the aft part of the arrestor hook. *National Archives and Records Administration*

The tail landing gear of the XTBD-1 is lowered. The wheel and tire were mounted with an axle pin secured with a hex lock nut on a caster at the bottom of a shock strut. Attached to the fairing are two shock cords, which acted to hold the fairing closed when the landing gear was retracted. On the production TBD-1, the retractable tail landing gear would be replaced by a fixed tail landing gear. *National Archives and Records Administration*

The arrestor hook, viewed from the starboard side, pivoted on an external mount forward of the tail landing gear. The tail is suspended by a rope attached to a pipe stuck through the hoist tube in the fuselage. The plug for the hoist tube hangs from a small chain. *National Archives and Records Administration*

The XTBD-1 had inflatable flotation bags in the wings above the main landing gear. They are shown inflated during a test of them on April 10, 1935. The bags were designed to keep the plane afloat long enough after a ditching for the crew to safely egress. *National Archives and Records Administration*

A dummy torpedo was mounted under the XTBD-1 on March 28, 1935, during the final fitting-out of the prototype plane, about two weeks before its first flight. The pronounced nose-down attitude of the torpedo is apparent; the torpedo fairing was not installed. *National Archives and Records Administration*

On the same date as the preceding photo, a 1,000-pound bomb was mounted on the two bomb racks. The opening between the racks had been covered with a fairing. The bomb was supported by two bands attached to the bomb racks. A white sway brace is present. *National Archives and Records Administration*

The area on the belly of the XTBD-1 where the torpedo was mounted in the preceding photo was reconfigured on the following day to mount two 500-pound bombs. On each side of the opening in the belly is a bomb rack; sway braces also have been installed. *National Archives and Records Administration*

Three 500-pound bombs are mounted on the belly of the XTBD-1 on May 11, 1935. Although it is hard to discern in the photograph, fairings are present between the tops of the forward bombs and the belly. This time, the bombs were attached directly to the shackles. Note the location of the third 500-pound bomb aft of the forward bombs, in a recess between the flaps. *National Archives and Records Administration*

CHAPTER 2

The TBD-1

After a period of testing of the XTBD-1 prototype, the US Navy proceeded to order 114 production planes, designated TBD-1. These were assigned Bureau Numbers 0268 to 0381. A subsequent order of fifteen more TBD-1s was assigned Bureau Numbers 1505 to 1519. A little over two years after the XTBD-1 had made its first flight, the TBD-1 undertook its first flight in May 1937. In general, the TBD-1 was quite similar to the XTBD-1 as modified with the tall canopy. The production planes were powered by the Pratt & Whitney R-1830-63 engine, rated at 900 horsepower. This photo from late June 1937 shows the first TBD-1, BuNo 0268. *National Archives and Records Administration*

The XTBD-1 was followed by 129 production TBD-1 aircraft, the first of which, Bureau Number 0268, was delivered in June 1937. This particular aircraft would spend its entire service life as a test platform, while subsequent aircraft would see fleet service.

The production aircraft differed from the experimental model in that all the test-driven modifications to the prototype were incorporated in the series aircraft from the outset. Additionally an improved and more powerful model of the engine, the R-1830-64, was used. The Pratt & Whitney was coupled to a three-blade, constant-speed Hamilton Standard propeller with a 10-foot, 3-inch diameter.

Beyond the previously mentioned changes, the production aircraft featured larger vertical tail surfaces and a redesigned lower cowling. As with the prototype, protruding through the right side of the cowling was a fixed .30-caliber machine gun. A .50-caliber M2 could be substituted in this position. A ring-mounted machine gun in the rear cockpit completed the Devastator's defensive armament.

A centerline rack was provided beneath the fuselage for either a torpedo or 1,000-pound bomb. Racks on each wing root could accommodate either a 500-pound general purpose bomb or six 100-pound fragmentation bombs.

The bombardier, who normal rode upright in the center cockpit, would lay prone beneath his and the pilot's position during bomb runs. A sighting window in the bottom of the aircraft allowed the bombardier to aim with the Norden bombsight. The sighting windows were covered by metal doors when not in use.

The torpedo was sighted by the pilot, using his windscreen-mounted telescopic gun sight.

Production of the aircraft can be broken into two large groups, the initial order for 114 aircraft, and an August 1938 order for fifteen further aircraft. The tail formation light on aircraft of the second order was positioned at the front base of the vertical stabilizer, as opposed to the port stabilizer position previously used.

Both the first and second production aircraft were utilized for testing. One of these, Bureau number 0268, the first production TBD, went to the Naval Aircraft Factory at the Philadelphia Navy Yard for conversion to a seaplane.

The Yard installed a pair of specially-made EDO floats, and modifications to the Devastator, now designated TBD-1A, were completed on August 14, 1939. It continued to be used in this role, first with the aircraft and then various torpedoes, being tested until September 22, 1943, when it was written off and unceremoniously scrapped the next day.

Production of the TBD-1 began at the Douglas Aircraft factory in Santa Monica, California, in 1936. A total of 129 production TBD-1s were produced, in two blocks of US Navy Bureau Numbers: 0268 to 0381 and 1505 to 1519. Here, TBD-1s are under construction at the Santa Monica plant. In the left foreground is BuNo 0300. Planes up to BuNo 0348 were painted in their USN colors and squadron markings at the factory. The first three planes to the left are in markings for Torpedo Squadron 2 (VT-2), with the squadron commander's plane the first in line with its red fuselage band. *National Museum of Naval Aviation*

TBD-1 fuselages are lined up on construction jigs at Douglas Aircraft. Rollover pylons with diagonal braces on their rears are visible on top of the structures. Numbers on small squares are affixed to the vertical tails; visible ones in the foreground run from 51 to 56. *Tailhook Association*

These TBD-1s under construction have their cockpit canopies and inner wing sections installed. Secured to the top of the wings on the first plane are slatted covers to protect the wing skin from scuffing and other damage. The horizontal tails have also been installed. *Tailhook Association*

In a frontal view of the first TBD-1, the new oil-cooler installation under the starboard wing is visible. This unit replaced the internal oil cooler in the starboard wing in the XTBD-1, which in turn had replaced the XTBD-1's original under-cowl oil cooler. *National Archives and Records Administration*

The wings of TBD-1 BuNo 0268 are in the folded position. Like the XTBD-1 prototype, the TBD-1 used hydraulic power to fold the wings, saving the trouble of having ground crewmen or flight-deck crewmen manually lower and raise the outer wing sections. *National Archives and Records Administration*

The TBD-1 eliminated the XTBD-1's abrupt angle in its profile from the bottom of the cowl to the forward part of the fuselage belly, having instead a straight profile line. Also, the TBD-1 had a single, redesigned carburetor air intake, on the starboard side only. *National Archives and Records Administration*

The wing flaps of TBD-1 BuNo 0268 are lowered. The flaps were of the split, trailing-edge type. They were hydraulically powered, and the pilot controlled them using a handle on the console to his right side. The ribs on the interior of the flaps are visible here. *National Archives and Records Administration*

When it left the assembly line at Douglas Aircraft's Santa Monica, California plant, the first TBD-1 was painted in an Aluminum finish. The national insignia, a White star with a Red circle in it on a Blue background, was on the top and bottom of each wing. *San Diego Air and Space Museum*

The lack of a carburetor intake on the port side of the cowl of the TBD-1 is apparent in this side view of BuNo 0268. A red navigation light was on the leading edge of the wingtip. A green navigation light was in the corresponding spot on the starboard wing. *National Archives and Records Administration*

Douglas TBD-1 BuNo 0268 displays a black, non-slip walkway along the wing root. The rear of the propeller blades near the hub were finished Aluminum, but a dark antiglare paint was applied partway up the blades, ending with several propeller-tip stripes. *National Archives and Records Administration*

The first TBD-1 is viewed from astern on June 28, 1937. The wings were a NACA 22 Series tapered design, while the horizontal tail surfaces were Modified N-69 design. The wings had a pronounced dihedral compared to the horizontal stabilizers and elevators. *National Archives and Records Administration*

Douglas TBD-1 BuNo 0303 is supported on tripods, probably for landing-gear tests, at the factory on January 19, 1938. Markings for plane 15 of Torpedo Squadron 2 are on the side of the fuselage aft of the wing, and the squadron insignia is below the windscreen. *National Archives and Records Administration*

A May 28, 1937, photo shows the panels removed from the starboard side of the cowl and the engine-accessories compartment. A Browning .30-caliber machine gun is mounted. Below the barrel of the gun is part of the carburetor air intake, with horizontal slats. *National Archives and Records Administration*

Components in the port side of the nose of the TBD-1 are visible with the panels removed. To the front is the Pratt & Whitney R-1830-63 engine. The exhaust is visible behind the open cowl flaps, aft of which are the oil tank (top) and engine supports. *National Archives and Records Administration*

The fixed .30-caliber machine gun installation on a TBD-1 is shown close-up in an April 22, 1938, photo. The gun was mounted on adjustable fittings to facilitate aligning it. Protruding through the windscreen is the pilot's Mk.3 Mod 2 telescopic gun sight. *National Archives and Records Administration*

The Browning .30-caliber machine gun M2 was fed from an ammunition box to its inboard side. On the rear part of the side of its receiver is the charging mechanism. Among other components above the gun is part of the engine bearing assembly. *National Archives and Records Administration*

A photo dated May 17, 1937, shows further details of the fixed machine gun mount. The charger has been removed from the side of the receiver. Below the receiver is the spent-cartridge ejector chute, which emptied through an opening in a fuselage panel. *National Archives and Records Administration*

The TBD-1 was powered by the Pratt & Whitney R-1830 Twin Wasp, a two-row, 14-cylinder, air-cooled radial engine of 1,830 cubic inch displacement. *National Museum of the United States Air Force*

The lower port engine-accessories compartment panel/engine-maintenance platform in this photo lacks black paint on the corrugated inner side. The locking handle on the outside of it was streamlined. Two hinged metal strips supported the panel when open.

The engine and the engine-accessories compartment to the rear of it with their cover panels removed are viewed from overhead on the port side of the TBD-1. Below the oil tank is a hinged panel with a corrugated inner surface, which doubled as a maintenance platform.

As viewed from the starboard side, the Mk.3 Mod 2 telescopic sight protruded through the windscreen and was mounted on two adjustable posts. A ring and bead sight was also on top of the telescope. Atop the instrument panel behind the telescopic sight is the Mk.24 torpedo director. *National Archives and Records Administration*

The Mk.3 Mod 2 sight and Mk.24 torpedo director are viewed from inside the cockpit. The Mk.24 torpedo director was a basic type of computing sight in which the pilot dialed-in the estimated size, speed, and distance of a ship to arrive at a drop solution. *National Archives and Records Administration*

The pilot's cockpit is viewed looking upward from the bombardier's station on the lower deck, giving a clear idea of how the lower instrument panel was spaced forward of the upper panel. At the center is the control stick, with the rudder/brake pedals to the bottom. *National Archives and Records Administration*

The pilot's cockpit of a TBD-1 is viewed from the starboard side. The curved left track for the pilot's sliding canopy is on the opposite side of the cockpit rim. The light area below the front of the seat is created by the bombardier's window with its doors open. *Tailhook Association*

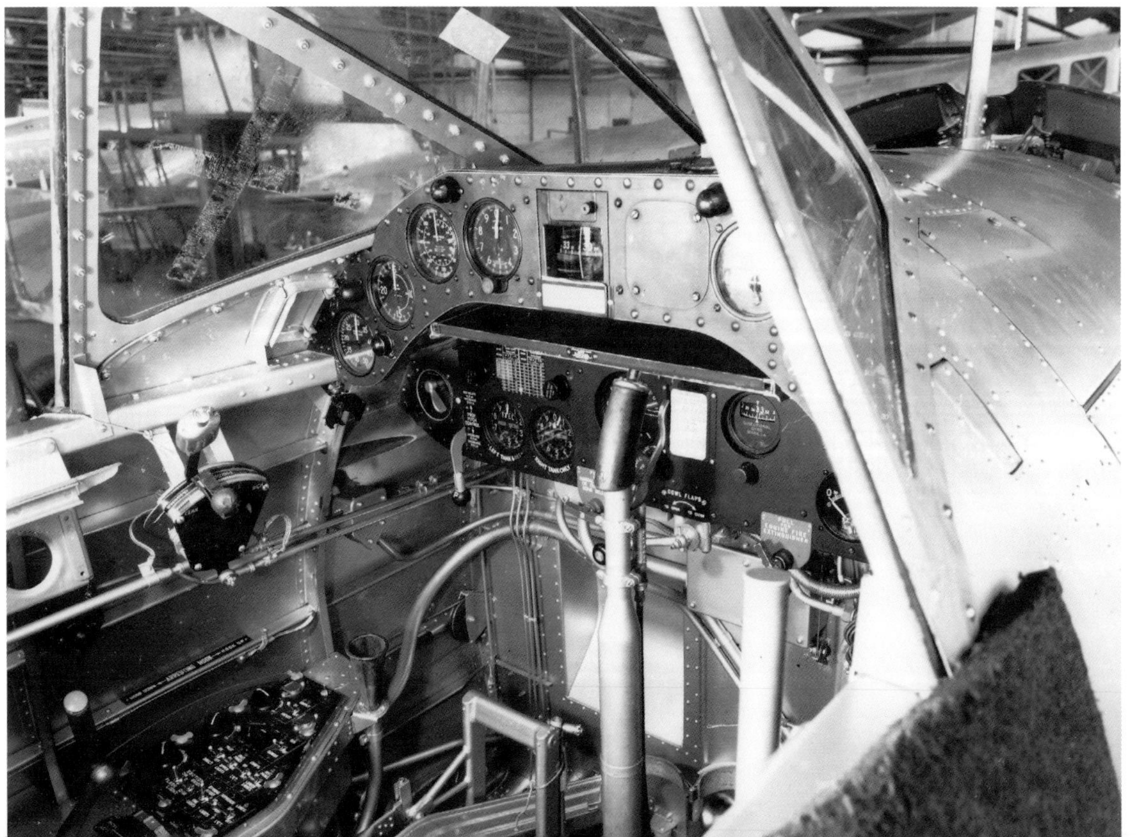

The pilot's instrument panel of the TBD-1 was quite similar in layout to that of the XTBD-1, depicted earlier. In this August 20, 1937, photo, the square instrument at the center of the upper panel is the compass. Visible between the upper and lower instrument panels is the rear edge of the sliding chart board. To the far left of the lower panel are the engine ignition switch and the propeller-pitch control. The small funnel-shaped object clamped to the side of the electrical panel on the port console is the pilot's relief tube. *National Museum of Naval Aviation*

In a view into the pilot's cockpit, below the control stick is the bombardier's window, with its doors closed. Directly below the pilot's port-side console is the bombardier's elbow rest. To the front right of the control stick is a fire-extinguisher bottle and valve. *National Archives and Records Administration*

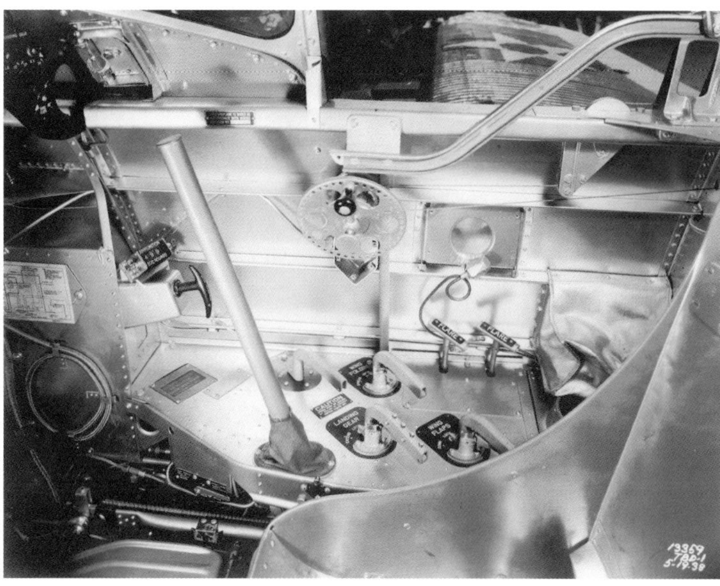

A May 19, 1938, photograph shows a much more pristine pilot's cockpit than the one in the preceding two photos. The interior was painted in Aluminum. To the left is the T-shaped charging handle for the fixed machine gun. Above it is the ammunition counter. *National Archives and Records Administration*

In this July 16, 1937, photo of a TBD-1 pilot's cockpit, safety belts are installed on the seat. At the upper center, aft of the throttle quadrant, is the pilot's radio/intercom control box. The pilot operated the arrestor hook with the tilted handle below the quadrant. *National Museum Naval Aviation*

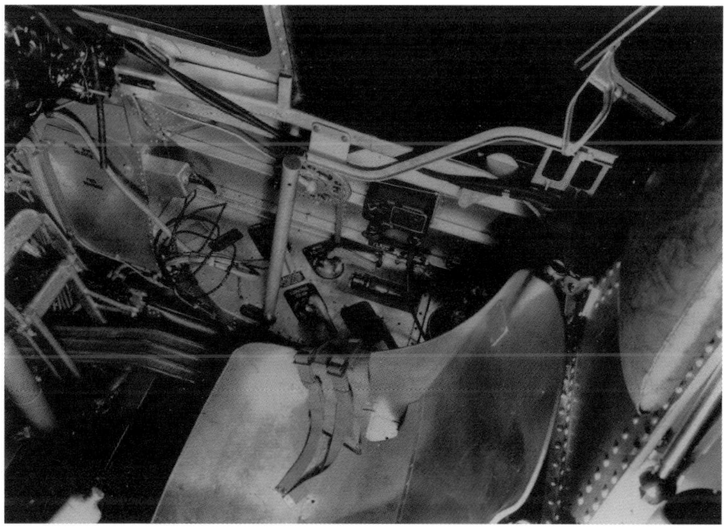

The same TBD-1 pilot's cockpit seen in the preceding photo is viewed from the port side. The right safety belt had a different configuration than the left one. The hand pump for the hydraulic system, used in the event of a power failure in the system, is at the center. *National Museum of Naval Aviation*

The assistant pilot/bombardier's cockpit also was painted with Aluminum dope. To the right of the seat is a CO_2 bottle and valve for inflating the wing flotation bags. On the wheel below the top edge of the cockpit was the hand crank for operating the canopy. *Tailhook Association*

In a view of the port side of the assistant pilot's cockpit of a TBD-1 dated July 16, 1937, the port rudder pedal is folded up, and below it is the footrest. On the console is the engine-starter crank and lighting controls, aft of which is an emergency rations box. *National Museum of Naval Aviation*

A different TBD-1 assistant pilot/bombardier's cockpit is observed from a similar perspective to the preceding photo. Adjacent to the CO_2 bottle is an oxygen bottle. Mounted above the CO_2 bottle is the assistant pilot's oxygen regulator, not present in the preceding photo. *National Museum of Naval Aviation*

The assistant pilot's cockpit in another TBD-1 was photographed from about the same angle as the preceding photo. To the lower right is a small button for releasing the assistant pilot's canopy, with a stencil over it reading "ENCLOSURE PRESS." *Tailhook Association*

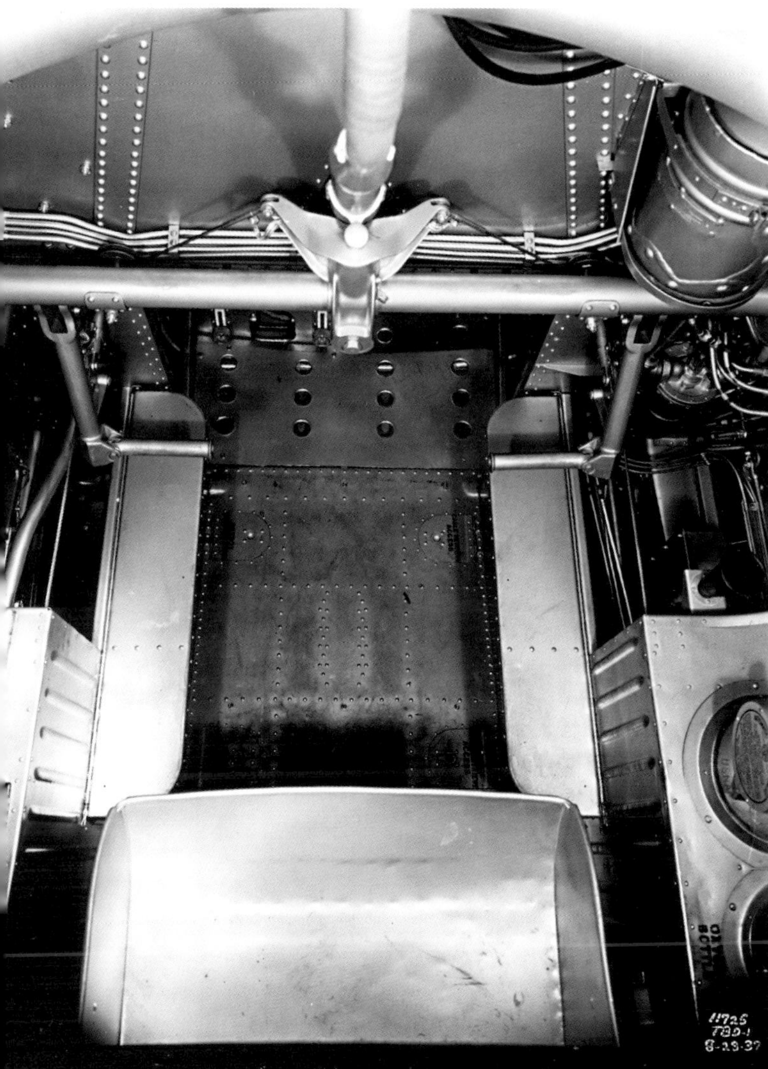

The assistant pilot/bombardier's cockpit of a TBD-1 is viewed from above in a photo taken in 1937. At the bottom is the bucket of the seat, to the front of which are the two footrests in the "down" (i.e., not stowed) position. To the sides of the seat are the consoles. Above the front ends of the footrests are the rudder pedals in their folded-down positions, ready for use. At the top center is the auxiliary control stick. *Tailhook Association*

On the TBD-1 the assistant pilot had a new instrument panel containing a compass, altimeter, airspeed indicator, and inclinometer on the rear of the rollover pylon. This replaced the assistant pilot's instrument panel in the XTBD-1, which was located in a lower position. *Tailhook Association*

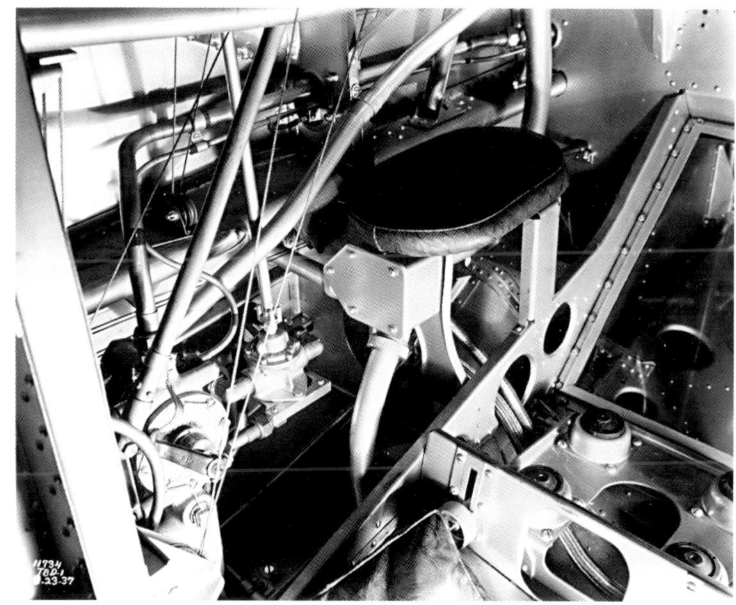

The bombardier's compartment in a TBD-1 is viewed toward its forward port corner. At the center is the bombardier's padded elbow rest. To the lower right is the buffered mount for a Norden bomb sight. To the far right is the left side of the bombardier's window. *Tailhook Association*

This is a continuation of the preceding photo, facing more to the right in the TBD-1's bombardier's station. To the left is the right side of the bombardier's window. To the center is the bombardier's switch panel. To the upper right are the bomb-selector levers. *National Archives and Records Administration*

A Norden bombsight is installed in the bombardier's station on the lower level of a TBD-1 in an August 16, 1937, photo. The Norden sight used high-quality optics and a mechanical computer to place the aircraft on the correct course to drop its bombs accurately. *Tailhook Association*

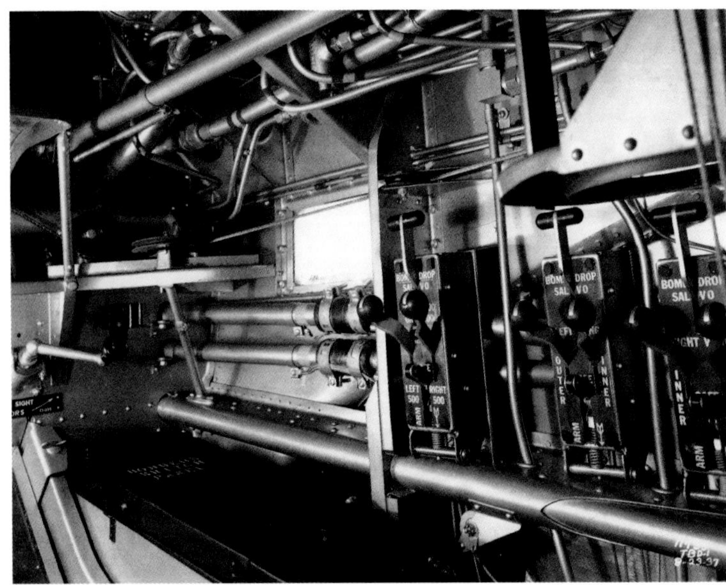

The cover for the bombardier's switch panel is closed in this view. The bomb-selector levers to the right allowed the bombardier to select which bombs were to be released, or if they were to be dropped all at once, in salvo. Arming switches were below the levers. *National Archives and Records Administration*

The Norden bombsight is turned to the side in a view up through the bombardier's window from below the TBD-1, with the bombardier's doors open. The window on the starboard side was hung on a piano hinge and could be opened, as seen here. *Tailhook Association*

Although this photo shows the radioman/gunner's cockpit in the XTBD-1 prototype, the layout was similar to that of the TBD-1, including the placement of the RDF antenna. The truck for the .30-caliber machine gun (not mounted) is to the left side of the ring mount. *National Museum of Naval Aviation*

This photo of the radioman/gunner's cockpit of a TBD-1 was taken about six months after the preceding photo. The truck is at the rear of the ring mount. On the sill to the lower right is a stencil indicating the location for a Type 26003-A radio transmitter key. *Tailhook Association*

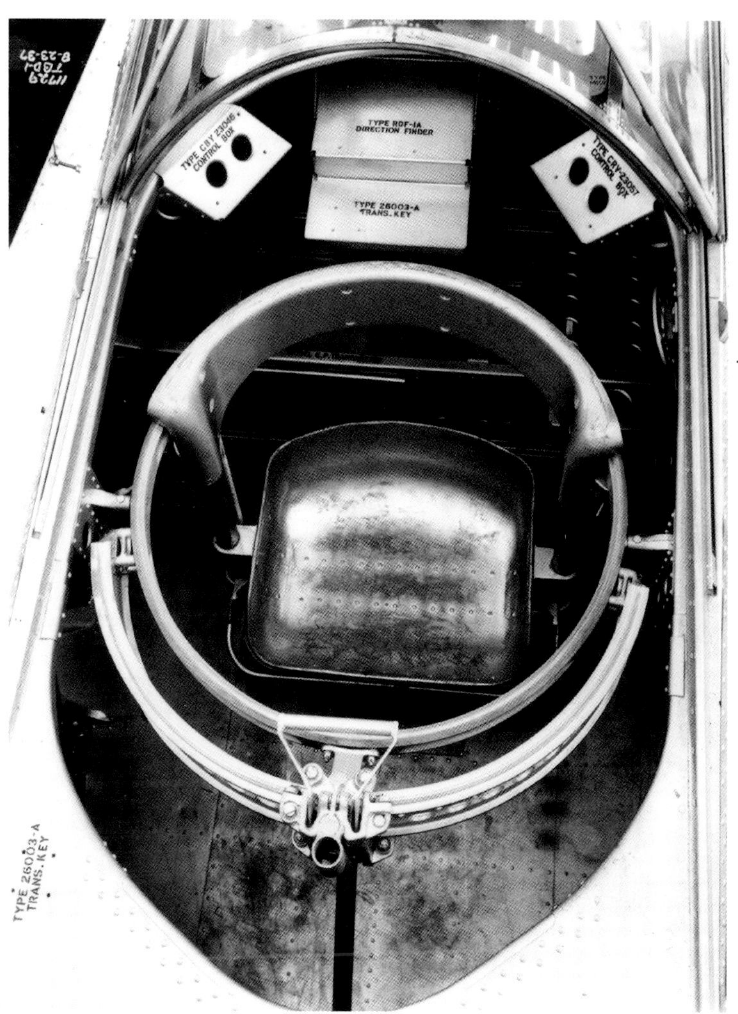

The TBD-1's ring mount and gunner's seat are viewed from aft. The socket in the truck at the rear of the ring mount was for inserting the .30-caliber machine gun cradle. The locking handle for the truck protrudes from the rear of the truck. The backrest of the seat rode on the ring mount and could be rotated on the mount, to allow the radioman/gunner to face aft when manning his machine gun, or face forward when operating the radio. Stencils indicating the locations of radio components are on the holders to the top. *Tailhook Association*

The starboard side of the radioman/gunner's cockpit is depicted in a July 16, 1937, photograph. The seat is rotated on the ring mount facing forward toward the radio equipment. Four marker flares are stored in holes in the floor to the right of center. *National Museum of Naval Aviation*

The port side of the radioman/gunner's cockpit is shown. To the upper left are the grips of the .30-caliber machine gun. The dark circle above the center of the photo is the reel for the trailing antenna, a wire antenna that was paid out behind the aircraft in flight. *National Museum of Naval Aviation*

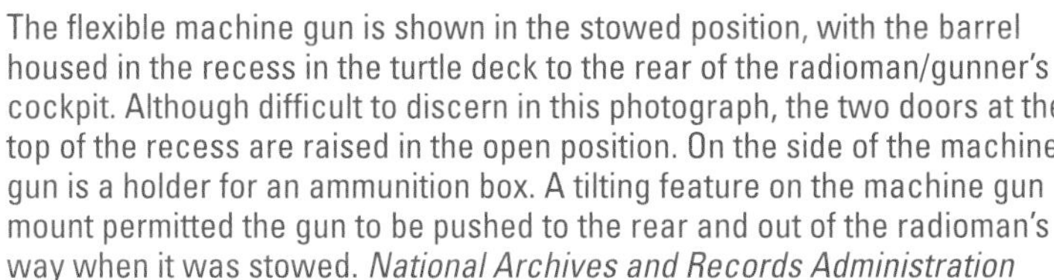

The flexible machine gun is shown in the stowed position, with the barrel housed in the recess in the turtle deck to the rear of the radioman/gunner's cockpit. Although difficult to discern in this photograph, the two doors at the top of the recess are raised in the open position. On the side of the machine gun is a holder for an ammunition box. A tilting feature on the machine gun mount permitted the gun to be pushed to the rear and out of the radioman's way when it was stowed. *National Archives and Records Administration*

The ring mount rested on a pivoting holder on each side of the aft cockpit. This allowed the radioman/gunner to use his legs and upper body to tilt the ring mount up or down, to achieve a better firing angle. Here, the gun and the ring mount have been elevated. The pivoting holder on the port side of the cockpit is just below the right side of the curved, perforated race, or track, of the machine gun mount. *Tailhook Association*

A flexible .30-caliber machine gun is in the unstowed, ready position. Fitted on the muzzle is a flash suppressor and a windage bead sight. The gun rests in a cradle, which pivots on a pintle mount that is inserted into the truck on the ring mount. *National Archives and Records Administration*

On June 30, 1937, an anti-spin sail, probably an experimental fitting, was photographed on a TBD-1 at Naval Air Station Anacostia. The anti-spin sail was attached to the arrestor hook and was intended to prevent the plane from entering a spin under certain conditions. *National Museum of Naval Aviation*

The tail landing gear on the TBD-1, unlike that on the XTBD-1, was non-retractable, but it was fitted with a shock strut, as seen here in a photo of the tail gear with its fairing removed. The shock strut is visible up in the fuselage, with a black data plate on it. *National Archives and Records Administration*

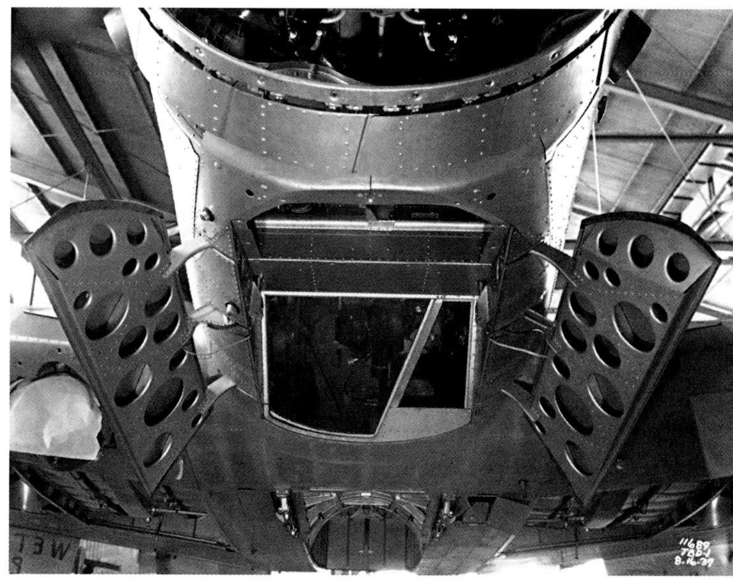

Originally, the doors for the TBD-1's bombardier's window had perforated inner linings and were hung on three hinges apiece, as seen in an August 16, 1937, photo. The bombardier operated the doors with a hand crank at the top right of his window. *Tailhook Association*

An Mk.XIII torpedo is secured to the belly of a TBD-1. A fairing above the torpedo lessened drag. The torpedo was secured in place by two cables fastened to the shackles on the bomb racks. To the top left is the oil cooler with its fairing removed. *National Archives and Records Administration*

The original doors caused buffeting when open, so the perforated liners gave way to smooth liners, and two hinges per door were now used, as seen in a May 19, 1938, photo. The fixed machine gun ejector chute outlet also was moved to the front of the window. *National Archives and Records Administration*

The Mk.XIII aerial torpedo was partially housed in a recess in the belly of the TBD-1. The most widely used US aerial torpedo in World War II, it had a length of 13 feet 5 inches, a diameter of 22.4 inches, and a speed of 33.5 knots (62.0 km/h; 38.6 mph) for up to 6,300 yards. *National Museum of Naval Aviation*

The first TBD-1, BuNo 0268, flies with a practice torpedo slung underneath on July 13, 1937. Markings consisted of the national insignia on the wings, "US NAVY" under the horizontal stabilizers, and the Bureau Number and aircraft model on the vertical tail. *National Museum of Naval Aviation*

A Douglas TBD-1 releases a torpedo during tests on July 23, 1937. The cables that had secured the torpedo to the bomb racks are hanging below the plane. The canopies of all three cockpits are open, and crewmen are visible in all three positions. *National Museum of Naval Aviation*

The TBD-1A was a one-off seaplane modification, created by adding floats to the first production TBD-1, BuNo 0268. At the Naval Aircraft Factory at the Philadelphia Navy Yard, steerable twin floats manufactured by the EDO Corporation were installed on the plane on August 14, 1939. The twenty-nine-foot-long floats were said to have been the largest ever installed on a single-engine aircraft. Although the plane performed adequately, it was relegated to use as a test aircraft before being scrapped in September 1943. *San Diego Air and Space Museum*

CHAPTER 3

VT-3, Fleet Service Begins

While the first two production aircraft were used for testing, the third aircraft was actually assigned for fleet service aboard the USS *Saratoga* (CV-3). The first TBD-1 to be used in fleet service was Bureau Number 0270, which along with 0271 and 0273-0291 were assigned to Torpedo Squadron 3 (VT-3). Under command of Lieutenant Commander (LCDR) M.E. Crist, the unit was assigned to Carrier Air Group 3, aboard the *Saratoga*. Noteworthy of the unit's prewar service, VT-3 conducted a successful simulated torpedo attack on the US fleet at anchor at Pearl Harbor in March 1938. While by early 1941, almost all of the fleet's TBDs had been painted in a somewhat austere overall light gray camouflage screen, three VT-3 TBDs continued to wear the colorful earlier schemes. The retention of the earlier yellow-wing scheme was the result of the aircraft being used in the filming of the 1941 movie *Dive Bomber*.

VT-3 moved to the USS *Yorktown* (CV-5) on May 30, 1942, replacing *Yorktown*'s own VT-5, which had suffered heavy losses at the Battle of the Coral Sea and was being rebuilt at Naval Air Station (NAS) Kaneohe in Hawaii with the new Grumman TBF-1 Avengers. During the Battle of Midway, only two of VT-3's Devastators (the aircraft being so named in 1940) survived the June 4 attack on the Japanese carrier *Hiryu*, led by LCDR Lem Massey. Both of the surviving aircraft were forced to ditch on their return to the US fleet when their engines quit. Following the devastating loss of aircraft at Midway, VT-3, like the other torpedo squadrons, was subsequently reequipped with the new Avenger.

In October 1937, the US Navy began equipping its aircraft carrier air groups with TBD-1s. First to receive these aircraft was Torpedo Squadron 3 (VT-3) of the USS *Saratoga* (CV-3), which conducted flight evaluations at NAS North Island, California, in the fall of 1937. Although the Bureau Number and the squadron/aircraft fuselage code are not visible on this TBD-1, it is thought to have been BuNo 0284, fuselage code 3-T-14, with a Willow Green upper half of the cowl, signifying the second plane of the 5th Section. *National Museum of Naval Aviation*

A TBD-1 of VT-3 prepares to take off from the flight deck of the USS *Saratoga*. The front of the cowl has a painted band, indicating that this was the plane of a section leader or the squadron leader. On the fuselage is the squadron insignia: a winged dragon on a torpedo. *National Museum of Naval Aviation*

TBD-1 BuNo 0288 of VT-3 rests at an Oakland, California airfield. Although it is difficult to discern it in this photo, the lower half of the cowl was painted Lemon Yellow, indicating that it was the third plane in the 6th Section. Each section consisted of three planes. *National Museum of Naval Aviation*

The same TBD-1 as in the preceding photo is viewed from a position farther forward. The propellers were painted Aluminum, with, from the tips inwards, Red, Yellow, and Blue stripes. The stripe on the vertical fin was a visual aid for landing signal officers. *National Museum of Naval Aviation*

A three-quarters aft port view of TBD-1 BuNo 0284 reveals the landing signal officer's (LSO's) stripe, the Bureau Number, and the aircraft model marked on the vertical tail. The LSO's stripe allowed the LSO to gauge if the aircraft's attitude was favorable for landing. *National Museum of Naval Aviation*

TBD-1s of VT-3 are secured with stays to the flight deck of the USS *Saratoga*. The nearest plane is 3-T-1, the squadron commander's aircraft; aft of it is 3-T-4. Just outboard of the black walkway along the wing root of 3-T-1 are the forward ends of a Red chevron. *National Archives and Records Administration*

On January 26, 1938, a TBD-1 lifts off from the *Saratoga.* The plane's individual number, 14, is visible on the starboard wing near the wing root, partially covered by the starboard horizontal tail. The chevron that extended over both wing tops was Willow Green. *National Archives and Records Administration*

A TBD-1 of VT-3 has just made an arrested landing on the *Saratoga*, and flight deck officers are motioning the pilot forward as another plane in the left background approaches for a landing. At the rear corner of the deck is the LSO's windscreen. *National Archives and Records Administration*

Wheels down, TBD-1 0370, assigned to VT-3, flies over a coastal city around the late 1930s. The arrestor hook has been painted with colored bands, probably White and Black. An "E" representing an award for efficiency is below the canopy. *National Museum of Naval Aviation*

TBD-1 3-T-4, BuNo 0275, was assigned to the leader of the 2nd Section of VT-3. As such, it wore a White fuselage band aft of the rear cockpit and a White band on the front of the cowl. In addition, the horizontal and vertical tail surfaces were painted White. *National Museum of Naval Aviation*

In 1940, the US Navy painted several aircraft in experimental camouflage design developed by artist McClelland Barclay, typically with Deep Blue and Dark Gray over White and Bright Blue. This TBD-1 of VT-3, photographed in August 1940, was painted in one such design.

By the time this TBD-1, BuNo 0339, with Barclay camouflage was photographed at NAS North Island in August 1940, the paint was deteriorating badly. The Non-Specular (matte) paints were water-based and suffered from lack of adhesion to the underlying paint. *Naval History and Heritage Command*

McClelland Barclay, designer of the disruptive camouflage scheme on this TBD-1, was a Naval Reserve officer and artist. Two squadrons, VT-3 and VT-5, tested the Barclay camouflage during fleet exercises in 1940, but it was not adopted for general use.

TBD-1s fold their wings during filming of the motion picture *Dive Bomber* at NAS North Island, California, in March 1941. In the foreground are TBD-1s of VT-3 in prewar colors, while behind them are VT-6 in the new Non-Specular (NS) Light Gray camouflage. *National Museum of Naval Aviation*

The TBDs of the 4th Section of VT-3, including 3-T-12 in the foreground, fly in formation. They are painted in the Non-Specular (NS) Light Gray camouflage scheme authorized on December 30, 1940, with national insignia on the fuselage sides. *National Museum of Naval Aviation*

Arrestor hook and landing gear extended, TBD-1 3-T-12 of VT-3 flies above ships of a naval force around 1941. The plane was painted overall in NS Light Gray. A Black LSO's stripe is painted on the vertical fin. The aircraft's number in the squadron, 12, is painted in small numerals on the front of the engine cowl. Standard practice during carrier takeoffs and landings was to have the cockpit canopy open, for quick egress in an emergency or crash. *National Museum of Naval Aviation*

In 1941, three TBD-1s of VT-3 proceed to their takeoff positions on the flight deck of the USS *Saratoga*, with Douglas SBD dive-bombers present aft of them. Faintly visible on the fuselage of the nearest TBD-1 just aft of the cowl is what appears to be the squadron insignia for VT-3. Along the centerline of the flight deck, flight deck officers motion to the pilots to keep them in their proper positions. These officers wore yellow jerseys and helmets. *National Museum of Naval Aviation*

CHAPTER 4

VT-2 Service

The second squadron to be outfitted with TBD-1s was VT-2 of the USS *Lexington* (CV-2), which began receiving them in January 1938, starting with BuNo 0292. By that spring, VT-2 had a full complement of 21 TBD-1s in its inventory. Here, the 3rd Section of VT-1 flies in formation around the late 1930s. The squadron insignia below the windscreens showed a bomb with a lit fuse riding atop a falling torpedo. The TBD-1s were painted in Aluminum, with Orange Yellow wing tops and Lemon Yellow tails. The section color on the cowls and the section leader's fuselage was True Blue. *National Museum of Naval Aviation*

The second squadron to be equipped with the Devastator was *Lexington*'s VT-2, which received Bureau Numbers 0292 through 0312 in December 1937. These aircraft joined *Saratoga*'s VT-3 in the mock attack on Pearl Harbor in March 1938.

On March 10, 1942, VT-2, flying from *Lexington*, along with *Yorktown*'s VT-5 struck Japanese transports in the Huon Gulf off New Guinea. The transports were part of the Japanese force invading Salamaua and Lae. The two squadrons launched twenty-three torpedoes, with one of *Lexington*'s TBDs scoring a direct hit on a Japanese 6,000-ton transport, sinking the vessel. Despite this strike and others by carrier-borne and land-based aircraft, which sank or damaged two-thirds of the transports, the Japanese invasion was successful.

The next confirmed hits by VT-2 flyers were on May 7, at Coral Sea. Having been located by US reconnaissance aircraft, *Lexington* (VT-2) and *Yorktown* (VT-5) launched twenty-two Devastators, as well as fifty-three Douglas SBD dive bombers, escorted by eighteen Grumman F4F Wildcats, against the Japanese light aircraft carrier *Shoho*. Trailing the dive bombers as well as their VT-5 counterparts, who had already hit *Shoho* with five torpedoes and thirteen 1,000-pound bombs, the Devastators of VT-2 delivered two more torpedoes into the hull of the hapless *Shoho* at 1129. Two minutes later Capt. Izawa ordered *Shoho* abandoned, the ship sinking four minutes after that.

The next day the Squadron lost its home when the Japanese sank *Lexington*, while VT-2 was unsuccessful at hitting the Japanese carrier *Shokaku* with even a single torpedo. One plane and crew were lost when they ran out of fuel returning to the US fleet, while twelve Devastators went down aboard *Lexington*.

Two TBD-1s from VT-2, the squadron leader's 2-T-1 to the left with red wing chevron and fuselage band, and 2-T-3 to the right, fly low along the Oahu coastline in 1938. The lower half of the cowl of 2-T-3 is red, in keeping with the third plane of the 1st Section. *Tailhook Association*

The 3rd Section of Torpedo Squadron 2 flies in a stacked formation over mountainous terrain. At the bottom is the section leader's plane, 2-T-7, with True Blue fuselage and cowl bands. The half-cowl section markings on the other two planes are visible. *Tailhook Association*

A formation of TBD-1s from Torpedo Squadron 2 was photographed in flight around 1938. In one of the vagaries of camera film and reproductions, the Lemon Yellow tail surfaces of VT-2 TBD-1s sometimes appear dark in tone and sometimes light. *National Museum of Naval Aviation*

Planes from two different sections of VT-2 speed above the waves around the late 1930s. The nearest plane had the last number of the squadron, 21. The other two planes were from the 5th Section, 2-T-13 and 2-T-14, and their section colors were Willow Green. *National Museum of Naval Aviation*

Some TBD-1s were fitted with a fixed .50-caliber machine gun instead of the .30-caliber machine gun, such as 2-T-17 of VT-2. The presence of a .50-caliber machine gun was indicated by the revised panel with a teardrop-shaped bulge aft of the carburetor intake. *National Museum of Naval Aviation*

The three TBD-1s of the 3rd Section of VT-2 make landfall over San Diego, California. The nearest plane, 2-T-9, was BuNo 0292. All three planes have mounts for a gun camera below the windscreen, and 2-T-8 has an "E" for efficiency award on the fuselage. *National Museum of Naval Aviation*

Nine VT-2 TBD-1s fly over a suburban area, most likely in southern California, in or around 1939. The fuselage codes on them are, on the left side of the photo, bottom to top: 2-T-1, 2-T-3, 2-T-7, 2-T-9, 2-T-13, 2-T-6. The fuselage codes on the three TBD-1s to the right of the photo are, bottom to top: 2-T-2, 2-T-14, and 2-T-5. *Tailhook Association*

Nine Douglas TBD-1s assigned to VT-2 fly in echelon in a photograph dated 1941. The closest four planes have visible fuselage codes: from the bottom they are 2-T-1 (BuNo 0300), 2-T-3, 2-T-2, and 2-T-7. The first two planes have the "E" for efficiency on the side of the fuselage below the pilot's cockpit canopy. All have the VT-2 squadron insignia below the windscreen. *National Museum of Naval Aviation*

CHAPTER 5

VT-5 Service

Assigned to the newly commissioned USS *Yorktown*, VT-5 began receiving its Devastators in February 1938. Deliveries were alternated between VT-5 and VT-6, established at the same time. Torpedo 5's first TBDs were Bureau Numbers 0313 through 0321, followed by 0331 through 0339, the nine aircraft in between being assigned to VT-6. Both these squadron's aircraft, like those of VT-2 and VT-3, were factory painted, even including unit and individual aircraft markings. Eight of VT-5's Devastators would be lost before Pearl Harbor, a result of mishaps and the hazards of carrier operations.

The squadron would first be committed to battle February 1, 1942, with an unsuccessful raid on Jaluit. Two Devastators were lost in a midair collision, while two more were forced down from fuel starvation. Following a no-hit torpedo attack on Japanese vessels in New Guinea on March 10, VT-5s TBDs armed with 100-pound bombs struck the Japanese seaplane tender *Kiyokawa Maru* of Lea, crippling the ship and also claiming a Japanese floatplane.

May 2, 1942, found three of *Yorktown*'s Devastators attacking, without success, the Japanese submarine *I-21*. Two days later the TBDs were back in combat, launching twenty-two torpedoes in the harbor of Tulagi, forcing a Japanese destroyer to run aground. One Devastator was lost, not due to enemy action, but from the failure of the radio and radio direction finder (RDF). On the seventh the torpedo bombers fared even better, putting five torpedoes in the *Shoho*, joining VT-2 in sending the Japanese carrier to the bottom of the Pacific. In June, the squadron converted to the new, larger TBF Avenger.

Established on July 1, 1937, at NAS Norfolk, Virginia, VT-5 was assigned to the USS *Yorktown* (CV-5) and began receiving TBD-1s in February 1938. When the squadron had received its complement of TBD-1s, they included Bureau Numbers 0313–0321, 0331–0339, and 1515. Here, some of VT-5's TBD-1s sit on the tarmac at NAS San Diego, California, in 1940. The squadron color of VT-5, Insignia Red, appears on the vertical and horizontal tail surfaces. The Orange Yellow on the tops of the wings continued under the leading edges of the wings, for purposes of smoother airflow over the wings. *Tailhook Association*

The leader of the 3rd Section of VT-5 banks his TBD-1, 5-T-7, BuNo 0331, to starboard. Emblazoned on the fuselage below the windscreen is an "E" for efficiency award. The "E" was White with Black shadowing. The bands on the cowl and the fuselage and the wing chevron were True Blue, the color of the 3rd Section of any US Navy TBD-1 squadron during the prewar years. *National Museum of Naval Aviation*

One of VT-5's TBD-1s flies over the arid hills of southern California around 1938. Prominent under the starboard wing is the oil cooler housing, outboard of which is the fairing for the landing gear strut. To the front of the "E" award is the squadron insignia. *National Museum of Naval Aviation*

With wings folded, some TBD-1s of VT-5 are assembled at NAS Norfolk. The one in the center, 5-T-4, BuNo 0319, has its engine-maintenance platform open. This was the 2nd Section leader's plane. To the left are the tails of several Curtiss BFC-2 Goshawks. *Tailhook Association*

TBD-1 5-T-14, BuNo 0335, of VT-5 was photographed at Oakland, California, in June 1939. This plane was the second one of the 5th Section, so the upper half of the cowl was painted Willow Green. A White LSO's stripe was painted on the vertical fin. *National Museum of Naval Aviation*

TBD-1 BuNo 0331 of VT-5 flies over Southern California on November 16, 1939. A close examination reveals a bulge-shaped fairing to the upper rear of the carburetor intake; it apparently was designed to give more clearance to the machine gun ejector. *National Museum of Naval Aviation*

Three TBD-1s of VT-5 run their engines at an airfield in Oakland, California, in June 1939. In the foreground is 5-T-4, BuNo 0319. To the left is 5-T-17, BuNo 0314, while to the right is 5-T-16, BuNo 0315. The black walkways on the wings were extra wide. *National Museum of Naval Aviation*

In this stunning 1940 color photograph are TBD-1s of USS *Yorktown*'s (CV-5) air group. In the foreground is BuNo 0381, the last of the Navy's original order of TBD-1s. This plane was assigned to VT-5's squadron leader, as signified by the Insignia Red bands, edged with black, on the front of the cowl and the fuselage aft of the rear cockpit. Insignia Red also was the tail color for *Yorktown*'s air group. The BT-1s in the background bear markings for Bombing Squadron 5 (VB-5). *Tailhook Association*

The aft end of the USS *Yorktown*'s flight deck is crowded with TBD-1s at NAS North Island, California, in May 1940. Three of these planes, including 5-T-14 at the starboard aft corner of the deck, have experimental camouflage schemes for Fleet Problem XXI. *Naval History and Heritage Command*

Aft of the island of the USS *Yorktown*, deck crewmen work to secure and remove TBD-1 5-T-11, Bu No 0284, of VT-5 after a landing accident on September 3, 1940. Damage to the aircraft was repairable, and all of the crewmen survived without suffering injuries. *National Museum of Naval Aviation*

Also suffering a landing accident on September 3, 1940—an unlucky day for VT-5—was BuNo 0297. Despite the severe crumpling to the fuselage and vertical fin, this plane was repaired and returned to service. It was lost in the Battle of Midway on June 4, 1942. *Tailhook Association*

After ditching alongside the USS *Yorktown*, TBD-1 5-T-15, BuNo 0336, is being recovered by an aircraft crane on the carrier. This Devastator, which was designated Plane C in the test camouflage for Fleet Problem XXI, had a mottled mix of NS Aluminum and an indeterminate dark color on the top surfaces and NS Aluminum on the balance of the surfaces. What appears to be a section of fuselage belly is hanging below the aircraft. *Tailhook Association*

Douglas TBD-1 5-T-14 appears without the test camouflage for Fleet Problem XXI shown in a preceding photograph. A feature that becomes apparent upon close examination of the photo and which is seen in other photos of VT-5 aircraft is that the non-slip wing walks along the wing roots were of two shades of black and wider than the norm. This may indicate that the wing walks were widened by the application of a darker shade of black on the outboard edge than the original black on the inboard side. *Tailhook Association*

A crewman, probably in a TBD-1, took this photo of TBD-1 5-T-13, BuNo 0334, speeding over the Bay Bridge between San Francisco and Oakland, with Yerba Buena Island to the left and Treasure Island to the right. The two-tone wing walk is visible. *Tailhook Association*

The *Yorktown* was transferred to the Atlantic in the spring of 1941, and VT-5's TBD-1s are seen here at NAS Norfolk in late 1941, in the camouflage scheme that replaced the colorful prewar paint: NS Blue Gray over NS Light Gray. In the background are SBDs. *National Museum of Naval Aviation*

After the December 7, 1941 Japanese attack on Pearl Harbor, the *Yorktown* returned to the Pacific. Here, a TBD-1 of VT-5 is parked in a revetment at NAS Kaneohe, Oahu. It is armed with a torpedo, and the undersides of the outer wing sections are NS Blue Gray. *Tailhook Association*

The 3rd Section of VT-5 flies in vee formation near San Diego, California in or around June 1941. The section leader flies at the front, with number 8 to his aft port quarter and number 9 to the aft starboard. All have the navy "E" for efficiency letter applied. *National Museum of Naval Aviation*

In another view of the 3rd Section of VT-5, the TBD-1s are flying line abreast, with the leader in the middle. The normal positioning for planes of a section was for the leader (plane 1) to be in the center, plane 2 (here, 5-T-8) to his port, and plane 3 to his starboard. *National Museum of Naval Aviation*

Including the plane this photo was shot from, there are five TBD-1s in this view. The one marked 6-T-16 was assigned to the leader of the 6th Section, and its wing and cowl bands and chevron were Lemon Yellow edged with Black. To the far right is 6-T-6. *National Museum of Naval Aviation*

At an unidentified desert airfield in the American southwest, TBD-1s of VT-6 are lined up for a pit stop. From left to right they are 6-T-6, BuNo 0327; 6-T-2, BuNo 0323; and 6-T-1; it's not clear if this was BuNo 0322 or its replacement after its crash, BuNo 0323. *National Museum of Naval Aviation*

In an early 1939 photo, the Bureau Number, 0322, is visible on the vertical fin of TBD-1 6-T-1, to the left. Following this aircraft are two other planes from Carrier Air Group (CAG) 6 from the USS *Enterprise*: an F3F-2 of VF-6 (top) and an SBC-3 of VS-6. All of Carrier Air Group 6's aircraft carried True Blue tails. *Tailhook Association*

As photographed at NAS Oakland, California, in August 1939, TBD-1 6-T-8, BuNo 0329, was fitted with a fixed forward-firing .50-caliber machine gun. The top half of the cowl was painted in the 3rd Section's color, True Blue. Subsequently, the .50-caliber machine gun was removed and a .30-caliber machine gun was installed to save weight. This plane later was lost in the Battle of Midway and its crew, Ens. Grant W. Teats, and ARM2c Hollis Martin, were killed in action. *National Museum of Naval Aviation*

The photographer moved a bit to his left to take this second photo of TBD-1 6-T-8, BuNo 0329, at NAS Oakland. The teardrop-shaped bulge in the access panel adjacent to the fixed .50-caliber machine gun is visible immediately to the front of the squadron insignia. *Tailhook Association*

On TBD-1 6-T-3, BuNo 0324, of VT-6 at NAS Oakland, in 1939, the white mark on the front of the vertical fin below the Bureau Number was the lower end of the LSO stripe. A full stripe was not necessary on this side because an LSO wouldn't see it from his station. *National Museum of Naval Aviation*

The wings are being folded and the assistant pilot/bombardier and the radioman/gunner can be seen going about their business in TBD-1 6-T-4, BuNo 0325, at Oakland, in June 1939. At the wing-fold joint, the wing bulkheads and components were painted Aluminum. *National Museum of Naval Aviation*

By early 1941, these TBD-1s assigned to VT-6 had lost their colorful prewar colors and now were painted in a drab camouflage scheme of NS Light Gray overall. The interiors of the wing-fold joints appear to have retained their previous Aluminum paint. *Tailhook Association*

A landing signal officer (LSO) holding his signal paddles watches as a TBD-1 assigned to VT-6 descends for a landing on the USS *Enterprise* around July 1941. The LSO was a critical player in flight operations on an aircraft carrier. Stationed at the port aft corner of the flight deck, with a canvas screen to shield him from the wind, he observed aircraft as they approached the carrier for landing, signaling them if they were approaching at the wrong attitude or were too high, too low, or just right. *National Museum of Naval Aviation*

TBD-1s of VT-6 crowded on the USS *Enterprise* on April 11, 1942, display a variety of markings sizes and placements. The Red and White rudder stripes and the large national insignia on the fuselage dated to a Bureau of Aeronautics directive of January 5, 1942. *National Museum of Naval Aviation*

A VT-6 TBD-1, 6-T-5, BuNo 0368, piloted by Ens. J.P. Gray, flies high above Japanese-held Wake Island during the February 24, 1942 raid. On this mission, VT-6's TBD-1s were used as level bombers; their 100-pound bombs had little effect except as a morale booster. *National Museum of Naval Aviation*